CELEBRITY BIOS

Britney Spears

Morgan Talmadge

Children's Press
A Division of Grolier Publishing
New York / London / Hong Kong / Sydney
Danbury, Connecticut

To J. Dewey, the other star born on December 2!

Book Design: Nelson Sa
Contributing Editor: Jennifer Ceaser

Photo Credits: Cover © Mitchell Gerber/Corbis; p. 4 © Reuters NewMedia
Inc./Corbis; pp. 6, 9 © ClassMates.Com Yearbook Archives; p. 11 © The
Everett Collection; p. 15 Above © Reuters NewMedia Inc./Corbis; p. 15
Below © Ethan Miller/Corbis; p. 16 © Lucia/Corbis; p. 19 © Fitzroy
Barrett/Globe Photos Inc.; p. 21 © AFP/Corbis; p. 23 © Andrea
Renault/Globe Photos Inc.; p. 25 © Reuters NewMedia Inc./Corbis; p. 26 ©
Reuters NewMedia Inc./Corbis; p. 29 © Fitzroy Barrett/Globe Photos Inc.; p.
31 © Henry McGee/Globe Photos Inc.; p. 33 © Alec Michael/Globe Photos
Inc.; p. 34 Above © Reuters NewMedia Inc./Corbis; p. 34 Below © Kelly
Jordan/Globe Photos Inc.; p. 37 © Lisa Rose/Globe Photos Inc.;
p. 41 © Reuters NewMedia Inc./Corbis.

Library of Congress Cataloging-in-Publication Data

Talmadge, Morgan.
  Britney Spears / by Morgan Talmadge.
    p. cm. (Celebrity bios)
  ISBN 0-516-23420-X (lib. bdg.) – ISBN 0-516-23582-6 (pbk.)
  1. Spears, Britney—Juvenile literature. 2. Singers—United States—
    Biography—Juvenile
literature. [1. Spears, Britney. 2. Singers. 3. Women—Biography.] I. Title. II.
  Series.

ML3930.S713 T35 2000
782.42164'092—dc21
[B]
                                                          00-031669

CONTENTS

CHAPTER ONE

Britney's Beginnings

"I want to be an artist that everyone can relate to—one that's young, happy, and fun!"
—**Britney on her official Web site**

Britney Spears may be the most amazing teen singing sensation ever! Her first album, . . . *Baby One More Time,* has sold more than eleven million copies. Her latest album *Oops! . . . I Did It Again* hit number one in its first week of release. It sold 1.3 million copies in just one week, making it one of the hottest-selling albums in the history of music. Her unique voice and incredible dance moves have earned

Britney is a talented performer who can sing, dance, and act.

Young Britney was involved in dancing and gymnastics.

her millions of fans all over the world. And it looks as though it won't be long before Britney takes on Hollywood!

Where did Britney get her many talents? Her story is not a Cinderella story or an overnight success story. Real talent and hard work have earned Britney the title "Princess of Pop."

A SMALL-TOWN GIRL

Britney Jean Spears was born on December 2, 1981, in the small town of Kentwood, Louisiana. Britney's father, Jamie, works in construction, and her mother, Lynne, is an elementary school teacher. Britney has an older brother, Bryan, and a younger sister, Jamie Lynn.

Britney developed her love for performing at a very young age. She sang "What Child Is This" at her church when she was just four years old. "She was always performing and belting out songs," her brother Bryan told *People* of his little sister.

Britney also began dancing when she was very young. She took ballet and tap lessons, and later, took tumbling and gymnastics classes. Britney practiced gymnastics up to 3 hours a day. At age seven, she won several state gymnastics titles.

Britney soon decided to give up gymnastics and focus on singing and dancing. She began entering talent contests that let her display her skills. Britney won singing competitions at Louisiana's Stars of Tomorrow and the local Kentwood Dairy Festival. She also sang in her church choir and at holiday shows at area shopping malls.

BIG APPLE BRITNEY

When she was eight years old, Britney tried out for "Mickey Mouse Club," a TV show on the Disney Channel. Britney was too young to get the part, but she impressed a producer at the audition. The producer helped Britney to get an agent, who would work to get her auditions.

Young Britney decided it was important to get the best training possible. So, she spent the next three summers in New York City, where she attended the Professional Performing Arts School and the Off-Broadway Dance Center. These schools provide young people with professional training in singing, dancing, and acting. In New York City, Britney lived with her mother and sister, while her father and brother stayed in Louisiana.

Britney was voted Most Beautiful in her junior high school.

Slowly but surely, the training was paying off. <u>When</u> she was ten years old, Britney won the title of Miss Talent USA. That prize got her the chance to compete on the TV show "Star Search." On the show, Britney won in her performance category on national television!

Britney went on to do many commercials. She also was getting more performance experience onstage. At age ten, Britney performed in an Off-Broadway musical called *Ruthless!* The show was based on a famous movie called *The Bad Seed*. Britney's character was a young girl who everyone thinks is sweet but who really does terrible things to people. "I was playing this really bad child," Britney remembers on her official Web site. "It was so much fun!"

MOUSEKETEER SPEARS

When Britney was eleven years old, she auditioned again for the "Mickey Mouse Club." This time, she got the part. The director of the "Mickey Mouse Club" told *People*, "No child had . . . the dance skills that Britney had." Britney was not the only talented performer on the show. Some of her costars were J. C. Chasez and Justin Timberlake of 'N Sync, Keri Russell of "Felicity," and the singer Christina Aguilera.

Britney moved to Orlando, Florida, and for the next two years she worked hard on the "Mickey Mouse Club." Unfortunately, during her second season on the show, it was canceled. Britney moved back to Kentwood to take a break. At age fourteen, Britney returned to school for her freshman year. Still, Britney was not able to forget the thrill of traveling and performing for audiences. On her official Web site, Britney recalled, "[High school] was fun

Britney was a cast member of "Mickey Mouse Club" for two seasons.

for awhile, but I started getting itchy to get out again and see the world."

STAR ON THE RISE

At age fifteen, Britney auditioned for an all-girl singing group. Britney realized, however, that she would rather be a solo artist (someone who sings alone). She recorded a demo tape (a music recording made to present a song to a record

label) and sent it to record companies in New York. The demo tape worked! In 1997, Britney got an audition with Jive Records, the same label the Backstreet Boys were on. Jive offered Britney a record contract and arranged for her to work with two music producers in Sweden. These producers were Max Martin, who worked with BSB and Ace of Base, and Eric Foster White, who had worked with Whitney Houston.

Together, Britney and her producers made an album that mixed danceable tunes (" . . . Baby One More Time") with ballads ("From the Bottom of My Broken Heart"). Britney also sang a cover version of the Sonny & Cher song "The Beat Goes On" and recorded a tune with a reggae beat, "Soda Pop." The album was titled . . . *Baby One More Time.*

After Britney finished recording the album in mid-1998, she made her first music video, for the single " . . . Baby One More Time." The original idea for the video had Britney playing a superhero character. Britney didn't like the idea at all, telling *Rolling Stone*, "I [didn't] want to be some Power Ranger." Instead, she came up with the concept of a group of schoolgirls with really hot dance moves. It also was Britney's idea to show off her bare stomach in the video. "The [schoolgirl] outfits looked kind of dorky," Britney explained to *People*. "So I was like, 'Let's tie up our shirts and be cute.' "

SPREADING THE MAGIC

Before Jive Records released . . . *Baby One More Time*, the label sent Britney on tour. For several months, she performed at shopping malls across the United States. Britney also toured as the opening act for 'N Sync. At first, 'N Sync fans weren't too sure about Britney, and Britney wasn't too sure about her performances, either. As she recalled in *Entertainment Weekly*, "I was so nervous because it was already out that a girl was opening up for 'N Sync. I'd walk out there and they would go 'Booo.' " It wouldn't be long, though, before the audience warmed up to Britney—"Once I'd start performing they'd go crazy."

Soon, Britney was gaining fans just on the strength of her live performances. Then, in October 1998, Jive Records released the single ". . . Baby One More Time." The song was an instant hit. It could be heard on radio stations across the country. The video for the single was a huge success on MTV. And when the album . . . *Baby One More Time* came out on January 12, 1999, it entered the pop charts at number one.

Britney Spears was just seventeen, and she had the number-one album *and* the number-one single in the United States. Britney had become a true pop star, and her life would never be the same.

Britney had once been the opening act for 'N Sync.

CHAPTER TWO

Slade Media Center

Fame and Controversy

"I love performing more than anything and having people hear my music."
—**Britney on her official Web site**

By mid-1999, Britney's record . . . *Baby One More Time* had sold more than six million copies. Yet fans weren't content with just listening to Britney's CD and watching her videos. They wanted to see the beautiful young woman and her amazing dance moves in person. They wanted to scream her name at concerts. They wanted to watch her sing the catchy grooves of "(You Drive Me) Crazy." So,

In the summer of 1999, Britney began a solo tour that took her all over the world.

in the summer of 1999, Britney decided to give her fans what they wanted—Britney live.

ON HER OWN

In June 1999, Britney kicked off a solo tour that took her all over the world. The tour was so successful that she began a second tour in January 2000 with LFO as the opening act.

Britney's touring schedule was exhausting. In March 2000 alone, Britney performed seventeen concerts in thirteen different states! Yet Britney can't imagine anything more rewarding than being on tour. In an AOL interview, Britney said, "I have to say that the best feeling in the world [is] to see all my fans singing the words to my songs . . . it's just so overwhelming."

PRINCESS OF POP

Britney had a very good year in 1999. Both her album and her tour were huge successes. She

Britney won a 1999 American Music Award
for Favorite New Pop-Rock Artist.

won the American Music Award for Favorite New Pop-Rock Artist and the Canadian MuchMusic Video Award for Favorite International Artist. She broke records by taking home four awards at the MTV Europe Music Awards. That year, Britney took home several 1999 Billboard Awards, including Female Artist of the Year and New Artist of the Year. She also was nominated for two Grammy Awards and two Blockbuster Awards.

WATCH OUT, BRITNEY!

Britney's busy life can be dangerous, too! In February 1999, Britney was rehearsing dance moves for the video for "Sometimes." During a dance move, Britney tore the cartilage in her left knee. She had knee surgery and spent a few weeks on crutches before she was able to dance again.

One year later, while filming the video for "Oops! . . . I Did It Again," another accident

Britney loaded up on four awards at
the 1999 MTV Europe Music Awards.

happened. A heavy camera fell and struck Britney in the head, giving her a concussion. Fortunately, after a day's rest, Britney was okay and was able to finish making the video.

BRITNEY FIGHTS BACK

By the end of 1999, Britney had sold an amazing nine million copies of . . . *Baby One More Time*. Along with all of the record sales came a great deal of publicity. Britney's face appeared on a number of magazine covers— including *Teen People* and *Entertainment Weekly*. But when Britney appeared on the March cover of *Rolling Stone*, she created a huge controversy. Britney was photographed lying on a bed in tiny shorts and a bra. She was holding a stuffed Tinky Winky doll and talking on the phone. It was a very sexy shot. Some people were so bothered by the photo that they boycotted (refused to buy) Britney's music. Britney, however, was not ashamed of the photo. "When you're an artist, you sometimes play a part," she explained to *People*.

Britney is inspired by other female performers, including Madonna and Mariah Carey, who aren't afraid to show their sexy side. When Britney went onstage to accept her award at the 1999 American Music Awards, many people were outraged at her choice of clothing. Britney's lavender-and gold-jumpsuit was open from the neck all the way down to her waist!

After performing at the 1999 MTV Video Music Awards, Britney had to deny rumors that she lip-synched.

Britney looked great in the outfit, but many people thought it was not appropriate for a young woman to wear. In *Teen People*, Britney defended the choices she's made: "I'm a Christian. I go to church. But my mom taught us, 'Don't be ashamed of your body. It's a beautiful thing.' "

In addition to a lot of bad publicity surrounding her sexy image, Britney has had to deal with a lot of gossip. She remained positive even as the press published a rumor that she had enlarged her breasts with surgery. The story was not true, but many people weren't convinced. At the 1999 MTV Video Music Awards, Britney found herself denying rumors that she and 'N Sync lip-synched during their performance together. *Time for Kids* asked Britney how she handles the negative opinions. "I just try to ignore it and go on," she answered.

At the 1999 American Music Awards, Britney's
revealing outfit caused a lot of controversy.

(I Can't Get No) Satisfaction
Oops!...I Did It Again
Lucky
One Kiss From You
Don't Let Me Be The last To Know
Don't Go Knockin' On My Door
Stronger
Where Are You Now
Can't Make You Love Me
When Your Eyes Say It
Dear Diary
What U See (Is What U Get)

CHAPTER THREE

Family, Friends, Fashion, and the Future

"I want music to always be a part of my life, and I just want to grow as a person each time each album comes out."

—Britney on *MTV*

Britney started working on her second album in the fall of 1999. She recorded the Rolling Stones's song "(I Can't Get No) Satisfaction." She worked with Shania Twain's producer on a song she wrote herself, called "Dear Diary." But the song that would become the first

Britney's album *Oops! . . . I Did It Again* hit number one on the pop chart in its first week of release.

single—and the title of the album—was "Oops! . . . I Did It Again." When the single was released in April 2000, it immediately hit the Top 20 on the charts. The album *Oops! . . . I Did It Again* entered onto the pop music charts in the number-one position. One month after the release of her album, Britney launched a summer tour that hit forty-four cities.

FAMILY

Britney may be a huge star, but what is most important to her is her family. When Britney is on tour, her family cannot always travel with her. Instead, a family friend named Felicia travels with Britney. Even so, Britney misses her family. She flies home to Kentwood as often as she can. At home in Louisiana, Britney still lives with her family. "I was thinking about getting a place in Los Angeles [but] I'm touring like crazy and I am not going to have the time," Britney tells *Entertainment Teen*.

Britney took her mother to the
42nd Annual Grammy Awards.

"When I have time off, I don't wanna be by myself and in my apartment. I am going to want to be with my mom."

FRIENDS

Britney misses her good friends in Louisiana as much as she misses her family. When Britney does get to see them, she said it's not much different than the way it used to be before she became famous. She told *Entertainment Teen* that she and her girlfriends talk about "what normal girls talk about, like boys and going out . . . shopping and clothes."

Britney also has found a good friend in Melissa Joan Hart, the star of TV's "Sabrina, the Teenage Witch." The two met when Melissa appeared in the video for Britney's song "(You Drive Me) Crazy," which was used in Melissa's movie of the same name. Britney also appeared on an episode of "Sabrina," in which she played herself.

Britney and Melissa Joan Hart are close friends.

DATING

Britney's one serious boyfriend was Jason Geddert, but they broke up in 1997. Yet there are many rumors floating around about whom

Britney is dating. Britney has been linked to many guys, including Justin Timberlake of 'N Sync. Both Justin and Britney deny those rumors, though. They have been friends since working together on "Mickey Mouse Club." There also has been gossip about Britney dating Prince William of England. Although the two have been e-mailing each other, Britney won't reveal whether they have met. "Right now I'm just having fun in my life," Britney revealed to *People*. "I don't have time for a serious boyfriend."

FASHION AND STYLE

Britney has great taste in clothing, makeup, and fashion. Her style is one of the things that make Britney so much fun to watch. Her fans know that if Britney likes something, it is guaranteed to look good on her. Britney explained to *Entertainment Teen*, "I don't really go with what's 'in' at the time. I go

Britney has modeled for
Tommy Hilfiger.

with what's flattering to me and what I think is cool."

Britney also likes to keep her eyes on the latest trends, so sometimes her style is very cutting edge. She likes MAC makeup, especially glittery shades. And though she's a natural brunette, she lightens her hair to a beautiful shade of blonde. She loves shopping for clothes at Banana Republic, BCBG, and Abercrombie & Fitch. Some of her favorite designers are Donna Karan, Betsey Johnson, and Steve Madden (for shoes). She has even modeled for Tommy Hilfiger.

33

A LIVING DOLL

Britney's great style also has influenced the creation of six different Britney Spears dolls. The Britney dolls were released in early 2000. Britney was very involved in the design of the dolls. Three of the dolls wear outfits from Britney's live concerts. The other three wear outfits from her videos, including "Sometimes," ". . . Baby One More Time," and "(You Drive Me) Crazy."

FANS

Britney's fans are incredibly loyal and are always happy to support whatever she does. Britney knows that without them, she would not be so successful.

All those fans can be a little scary, though. Sometimes they even get out of hand. Britney and her mom were once mobbed at a mall when they were just trying to shop. Britney told *Entertainment Weekly*: "It's flattering to a

Although Britney is a huge pop star, she always takes the time to sign autographs for her many fans.

certain extent, but sometimes [fans] get a little overbearing!" Still, Britney is almost always happy to sign an autograph. She knows that some of her fans wait for hours to see her in person.

Family, Friends, Fashion, and the Future

Britney has some unusual fans, too. One male fan in Los Angeles entered a Britney look-alike contest. He looked so much like her that he won! As part of his prize, he got to meet Britney at one of her concerts.

Britney is a star who is really interested in getting to know her fans. One way that she does this is by using the Internet. (. . . *Baby One More Time* even includes a song called "E-mail My Heart"!) AOL once hosted an event during which fans could chat online with Britney. More than 200,000 fans logged on for the chat!

GIVING BACK

Britney knows that she has been very lucky to be in her position. She has spent time thinking of ways that she could share her good fortune with others. Britney did a photo shoot for the Milk Mustache campaign in 1999. The ad encouraged young girls to make sure

Britney is very involved in charity causes. Here, she announces the creation of The Britney Spears Foundation.

Did you know?

Britney will sometimes disguise herself in a wig, hat, and glasses so that she won't be recognized on the street.

they are getting enough calcium in their diets.

Britney also is committed to working for different charity causes. She visits cancer patients in the hospital. In early 2000, she established The Britney Spears Foundation. The foundation organizes a summer camp for underprivileged young people who want to be performers. The two-week camp will feature dancers, singers, and acting teachers. Britney hopes to spend time with the campers if her schedule is not too busy.

In May 2000, Britney kicked off a world tour to support the album *Oops! . . . I Did It Again*. The tour started in Columbia, Missouri, and took her around the globe, ending in Paris, France. That summer, Britney also recorded a TV special, "Britney in Hawaii," which aired on

Fox. The show featured Britney performing and hanging out in Hawaii.

Britney's many talents were showcased in 2000. Nickelodeon awarded her the Favorite Female Singer award at the Nickelodeon Kids' Choice Awards. Britney was given the chance to stretch her acting muscles as the host and musical guest on "Saturday Night Live." She also cowrote a book with her mom, Lynne, called *Heart to Heart*. The book hit the stores in May.

Britney's hometown is so proud of her success that they are opening a museum in her honor. The Britney Spears Museum is scheduled to open in Kentwood, Louisiana, in 2001.

THE FUTURE

All of Britney's years of practicing and performing have paid off. She has sold millions of albums. She has fans all over the world and has many awards to show for her music. There is one thing on the minds of all Britney's fans. What will she do next?

"I really want to do a movie," Britney told *Teen People*. You can bet that she's thinking about a flick with one of her favorite male stars. When *Time for Kids* asked Britney what kind of movie she would like to star in, she replied, "A movie with Ben Affleck as the leading guy!" Britney also has talked about attending college someday.

Whatever Britney chooses to do, it's sure to be a success. Britney's talents have made her a star, and she has inspired many young people to follow their own hopes and dreams. During an AOL online chat, Britney encouraged teens to "go for what you believe in and stay confident with yourself." Good advice, from one of the today's most successful and beautiful young stars!

Britney often talks with her fans before a concert.

TIMELINE

1981	• Britney was born on December 2 in Kentwood, Louisiana.
1991	• Britney wins the title of Miss Talent USA. • Britney wins in her performance category on the TV show "Star Search." • Britney acts in the Off-Broadway musical *Ruthless!*
1992	• Britney joins the cast of "Mickey Mouse Club."
1997	• Britney gets an audition and signs a record contract with Jive Records. • Britney goes to Sweden to record her first album. • Britney dates Jason Geddert.
1998	• Britney tours, performing in shopping malls across the United States. • Britney opens for 'N Sync on their tour. • In October, the single ". . . Baby One More Time" is released.
1999	• The album . . . *Baby One More Time* and the single " . . . Baby One More Time" both hit number one on the pop music charts.

1999
- Britney goes on tour with opening act LFO.
- Britney is named one of *Teen People's* "21 Hottest Stars Under 21."
- Britney is voted one of *People's* "50 Most Beautiful People."
- Britney wins an American Music Award for Favorite New Pop-Rock Artist.
- Britney takes home four awards at the MTV Europe Music Awards.
- Britney wins Female Artist of the Year and New Artist of the Year at the 1999 Billboard Awards.

2000
- The Britney Spears Foundation is established.
- In May, *Oops! . . . I Did It Again* hits number one on the music charts.
- Britney's book *Heart to Heart* hits bookstores.
- Britney begins her summer tour
- Britney hosts NBC-TV's "Saturday Night Live."
- Britney's TV special "Britney in Hawaii" airs on the Fox network.

Name	Britney Jean Spears
Nickname	Brit-Brit
Born	December 2, 1981
Birthplace	Kentwood, Louisiana
Family	Mother: Lynne; Father: Jamie; Brother: Bryan; Sister: Jamie Lynn
Hair/Eyes	Brown (dyed blonde)/Brown
Sign	Sagittarius
Pets	Mitzi (Yorkshire terrier); Kane (rottweiler); Lady (poodle)

Favorites

Car	Mercedes
Food	Pasta, hot dogs, cookie-dough ice cream
Music	Whitney Houston, Mariah Carey, Michael Jackson, Goo Goo Dolls, Madonna
Book	*The Horse Whisperer*
Author	Jackie Collins
Actors	Ben Affleck, Brad Pitt
TV Show	"Dawson's Creek"
Clothing	sunglasses, Skechers shoes, sweatshirts
Season	summer

album a recording of different musical pieces

audition a tryout; to perform in order to get a role

autobiography a book about a person as told by the person

boycott refuse to buy

charity aid given to those in need

chat room an online discussion group on the Internet

controversial something that causes differing viewpoints

criticism an opinion—usually a negative one

demo tape a music recording made to present a song to a record label

director someone who is in charge of directing a TV show, movie, or music video

musical a play with singing and dancing

producer a person who supervises the production of a record

single a song that is released separately from an album

solo artist someone who sings alone

tour a series of concerts or appearances

FOR FURTHER READING

Peters, Beth. *True Brit: The Story of Singing Sensation Britney Spears.* New York: The Ballantine Publishing Group, 1999.

Robb, Jackie. *Britney Spears: The Unauthorized Biography.* New York: HarperCollins Publishers, 1999.

Spears, Britney and Lynne Spears. *Britney Spears' Heart to Heart.* New York: The Crown Publishing Group, 2000.

Strauss, Alix. *Britney Spears.* New York: St. Martin's Press, 1999.

Britney.com
www.peeps.com/britney/home.html
This is a Web site sponsored by Jive Records, Britney's record label. It includes audio clips, e-mail updates, photos, excerpts from her book *Heart to Heart*, and the latest tour information.

The Official Britney Spears Web Site
www.britneyspears.com
Britney's mom, Lynne, keeps fans up-to-date on the events in Britney's life and answers many of their questions. Fans also can check the tour dates, see pictures of Britney, or join chat rooms to talk about her. You can even buy clothes, dolls, CDs, and Britney's autobiography *Heart to Heart* at the Britney Boutique!

You can write to Britney at the following address:
Britney Spears
c/o Elephant Walk Entertainment
9200 Sunset Boulevard, Suite 430
Los Angeles, CA 90069

ABOUT THE AUTHOR

Morgan Talmadge is a freelance writer and soccer coach living in Mt. Vernon, Iowa.